DATA! DIALOGUE! DECISIONS!

D0874838

In A Nutshell

s e r i e s

DATA! DIALOGUE! DECISIONS!

The Data Difference

WAGGONER LIBRARY
DISCARD

In A Nutshell

collection

WAGGONER LIBRARY
TREVECCA NAZARENE UNIVERSITY

Brian M. Pete • Catherine A. Duncan

CORWIN
A SAGE Company

Copyright © 2004 by Corwin

All rights reserved. When forms and sample documents are included, their use is authorized only by educators, local school sites, and/or noncommercial or nonprofit entities who have purchased the book. Except for that usage, no part of this book may be reproduced or utilized in any form or by any means, electronic or mechanical, including photocopying, recording, or by any information storage and retrieval system, without permission in writing from the publisher.

For information:

Corwin
A SAGE Company
2455 Teller Road
Thousand Oaks,
   California 91320
(800) 233-9936
Fax: (800) 417-2466
www.corwinpress.com

SAGE Ltd.
1 Oliver's Yard
55 City Road
London EC1Y 1SP
United Kingdom

SAGE India Pvt. Ltd.
B 1/I 1 Mohan Cooperative
   Industrial Area
Mathura Road,
   New Delhi 110 044
India

SAGE Asia-Pacific Pte. Ltd.
33 Pekin Street #02-01
Far East Square
Singapore 048763

Printed in the United States of America

A catalog record of this book is available from the Library of Congress.

ISBN: 978-0-9717-3329-9

This book is printed on acid-free paper.

09   10   11   12   13   10   9   8   7   6   5   4   3   2   1

Dedication

To my wife, Robin, who helps me see how far I can go if I just keep showing up.

Brian M. Pete

To my parents, Jack and Ruthann Sambo, who always believed in me, and David Kinney, boss, friend, mentor.

Catherine A. Duncan

Contents

■ □ ■ □ ■

■ □ ■ □ ■

Preface

The Coaches' Meeting ...

The following conversation between three basketball coaches illustrates the difference between process-driven and results-driven solutions. Later in the book, this conversation is examined in detail.

VARSITY COACH. I have been looking over the stats for this year and comparing them to last year. You know what I see?

ASSISTANT COACH. We were better last year.

VARSITY COACH. Yes, but do you know why?

ASSISTANT COACH. We won more games last year.

VARSITY COACH. Brilliant observation ... I know we won more games last year, but I noticed something else in the statistics. Something besides wins and losses.

FRESHMAN COACH. I think what you mean is rebounding. We out-rebounded the other team in every game we won.

VARSITY COACH. Exactly, rebounding. This year we are not rebounding. Get rebounds and you get the wins, it's that simple.

ASSISTANT COACH. We had taller players last year. Rebounds come off the rim, the rim is high, tall players have an advantage. Tall players make better rebounders. You tell me how to get kids to grow and our rebounding will improve. When our rebounding improves, we'll win more games.

FRESHMAN COACH. But, when you look deeper into the statistics, you see that our big guys always rebounded about equal to the other team's big guys. It was our guards who got the rebounds in the victories. The short quick players get the rebounds that matter.

ASSISTANT COACH. I'd like to see who got the rebounds in the losses, and I would also like to see how other teams rebounded against us versus how they rebounded against other people.

FRESHMAN COACH. OK, sure, and then I could go back a couple years and compare those numbers to the numbers of the best teams in the state by running an analysis on a spreadsheet program on my computer.

VARSITY COACH. Now wait a minute. We want to improve our win–loss record. I don't think we have to crunch numbers like Price Waterhouse to do that. I have been coaching for 18 years, you about 13, and you 10. If, between us, we can't figure out how to improve out team, we are in sorry shape.

ASSISTANT COACH. What do you mean, Coach?

VARSITY COACH. Let's look at the numbers that tell us when we rebounded well and when we didn't. Let's look at our practice schedule and see when we worked on rebounding. If we do not emphasize rebounding in practice, how can we expect the kids to do it during the game?

FRESHMAN COACH. I got a great drill to teach technique, and the kids can do the drill on their own.

ASSISTANT COACH. I think if we tell the kids what we want them to do, really make it clear why it is important to the team …

VARSITY COACH. Until they understand, let's have them set some goals. Every kid has to get five rebounds a game.

ASSISTANT COACH. In the next game?

VARSITY COACH. OK, maybe too much too soon. How about, three games from now every kid will get at least five rebounds a game and we, as a team will out-rebound every opponent the rest of the season.

FRESHMAN COACH. Well, we said rebounding leads to victories, so this seems like a plan.

ASSISTANT COACH. If it doesn't get the results we want, then we'll try something else.

Introduction

Teacher-student teams have existed from the beginning of learning. Socrates and Plato, Mary Sullivan and Helen Keller, and Dr. Higgins and Eliza are just a few well-known combinations that produced notable learning on the part of the students. The goal for each of these teams was for the learner—Plato, Helen Keller, Eliza—to learn. Notice that the goal does not mention teachers teaching. So, if the goal is for the student to learn, and it is the student who actually does the learning, what contribution did the teacher make to these duos' goals?

> **The teacher enables, facilitates, encourages, goads, spurs, prompts, cheers, persuades, challenges, leads, steers.**

The teacher enables, facilitates, encourages, goads, spurs, prompts, cheers, persuades, challenges, leads, steers, ... well, the idea is clear. Teachers afford (make possible or allow) the act of learning by another. They set the learning climate, scaffold processes, assess achievements, encourage reflection, and model behavior—all in pursuit of helping students to learn.

"The teacher is also the student" is a very apt characterization of how teachers meet the many responsibilities of their role in the teacher-student duo. They become lifelong learners—always asking questions, seeking answers, and trying new things so that they may keep abreast of changes that influence student achievement, whether from inside or outside the school walls.

■□■□■

What's It All About?

It is well known that quality teachers can make the difference in terms of increasing student achievement (Haycock, 1999). Schools under pressure from local, state, and national administrators to produce measurable results have turned to teachers, asking them to work with accurate current data to raise the level of achievement for all students.

What has brought about the change in attitude? Viadero (2000) has pointed out that there is an achievement gap. The achievement gap is about poverty, race, expectations, teacher quality, parenting and test bias. But, in the end, it is about literacy instruction...when kids can't, don't, or won't read, it affects everything else they do.

Figure Intro.1 shows some facts that clearly delineate a student achievement gap; Figure Intro.2 displays a few remarks about the effects of the gap; and Figure Intro.3 shows some efforts that have reduced the gap.

Defining the Achievement Gap

- Only 1 in 50 Latinos and 1 in 100 African American 17-year-olds can read and gain information from specialized text, such as the science section in the newspaper. Source: Haycock, 2001, p. 7.

- There is a 30% illiteracy rate across American schools. Source: Joyce, 1999, p. 129.

- The fourth-grade reading slump is a myth. It's a slow decline, getting further behind. Source: Barbara Taylor, personal communication, 12 July 2003.

- Parents with professional jobs speak about 2,153 words an hour to their toddlers; those in poverty only about 616. A five-year-old child from a low-income home knows 5,000 word, while a middle-class child already knows 20,000 words. Source: Hart and Risley, 2003.

- Students entering high school in the 35 largest cities in the United States read at the sixth-grade level. Students not reading at grade level are included in the achievement gap. Source: Vacca, 2002, p. 9.

- Achievement on literacy hasn't risen for 70 years. Source: Joyce, 1999, p. 129.

- U.S. students: the longer they are in school, the further they fall behind the averages of other countries. Source: Joyce, 1999, p. 129.

- 90 million Americans lack basic literacy skills, with consequences for poverty, welfare, employment status, and crime. Source: U.S. Department of Education, 1993.

Figure Intro.1

Checking the Effect of the Gap

- 40% of all *mathematics* errors on state tests are reading errors. Source: Joyce, 1999, p. 129.

- There is no sixth grade math test ... it's cumulative; it's is a 6, 5, 4, 3, 2, 1 test. Source: Barbara Taylor, personal communication, 12 July 2003.

- 80% of the boys in middle school prefer non-fiction. Source: Barbara Taylor, personal communication, 12 July 2003.

- Reading: Elementary School: 90% narrative text; High School, 90% informational text. The change in the type of reading affects the students' scores. Source: Barbara Taylor, personal communication, 12 July 2003.

- Informational text for Grade 1: 3% of reading (2.6 min./day); in Grades 2 to 5, 19% of reading. The amount of time spent reading informational text impacts student achievement. Source: Taylor, Pearson, Peterson, and Rodriguez, (in press).

- A high school chemistry text can include 3,000 new vocabulary terms—more words than students are expected to learn in foreign language classes. Reading science texts requires additional reading skills that students may not have used in other content areas. Source: Barton, Heidema, and Jordan, 2002, p. 25.

- Algebra II is the new civil right. It's the threshold course. It more than doubles the odds that a student who enters postsecondary education will complete a bachelor's degree. The achievement gap will continue to grow unless more minority students participate in Algebra II courses. Source: Carnavale, 2003, p. 14.

- Thirty-two states and the District of Columbia still do not release test scores by subgroups. Knowing the large gap separating students from different subgroups will be a call to action for educators. Source: Gehring, 2002, p. 2.

- American businesses lose $60 million a year due to lack of employees' basic reading skills. Source: U.S. Department of Education 1993.

- ***Speaking*** is the number one skill for getting a job. Reading, writing, listening, and speaking skills are needed in the work place. Speaking is often overlooks and is critical for job interviews.

- 50% of high school dropouts are unemployed. Source: Schmoker, 1999b, p. 4.

- 68% of the all prisoners are high school dropouts. Source: Schmoker, 1999b, p. 3.

- The State of Indiana bases projections for future prisons on number of second graders ***not reading*** at grade level. Source: Schmoker, 1999b, p. 4.

- The only behavior measure that correlated significantly with reading scores is the number of books in the home; 61% of low-income families have no books at all in their homes. Source: U.S. Department of Education 1993.

Figure Intro.2

Reducing the Gap

- Literacy is vital to all subjects. Reciprocally, all subjects can enhance literacy. Source: Joyce, 1999, p. 129.

- Milwaukee Public Schools: 90% minority, 90%disadvantaged, but 90% at or above national norms in reading and mathematics. Source: Schmoker, 1999b, p. 1.

- Noticeable effects from 25 to 30 minutes of independent reading every day. The more time students spend independently reading, the greater the positive effect on student achievement. Source: Taylor, Pearson, Peterson, and Rodriguez, in press.

- Ten years ago, Kentucky was the first state to embrace standards-based reform. In reading, 7 of the 20 top-performing elementary schools are high-poverty schools. Source: Haycock, 2001, p. 4.

- "What schools do matters enormously. And what matters most is good teaching. Not as previously believed that what student learned was largely a factor of their family income or parental educations, not of what schools did." Source: Haycock, 2001, p. 6.

- "High student achievement correlates very strongly with strong administrative leadership, high expectations for student achievement, an orderly atmosphere conducive to learning, an emphasis on basic skill acquisition, and frequent monitoring of student progress. Source: Cawelti, 2003, p. 19 summarizing R. Edmond's work.

Figure Intro.3

This change in attitude has reached the federal level. Now, the federal government mandates this shift in focus from "process-driven" to "results-driven." Classroom teachers have a wonderful chance to do what they are uniquely trained to do—make instructional decisions in their classroom.

What the U.S. Department of Education says ...

The Department of Education is changing education to make it an evidence-based field. The goal is being accomplished by dramatically improving the quality and relevance of research funded or conducted by the Department, by providing policy makers, educators, parents, and other concerned citizens with ready access to syntheses of research and objective information that allow more informed and effective decisions, and by encouraging the use of this knowledge. (U.S. Department of Education, 2003)

Results-driven change means, simply, if something works, if it changes the level of achievement in the classroom, if there is evidence that children are learning, then continue. But if there is no change or less gains, then do something different, do something different quickly, and do it with the cooperation of the classroom teacher.

A key to results-driven change is responding rapidly to results. As Joyce, Wolf, and Calhoun say, "...where significant improvement has happened, it has happened rapidly... Innovations can be implemented and gains seen in student achievement within a year" (quoted in Schmoker, 1996, p. 51). Furthermore, "They insist...that the key is to pay attention to already existing approaches that work and work fast" (p. 51).

■ □ ■ □ ■

What's the History of Results-Driven Change?

Outside the Educational World

Business

Education is not the first profession to be influenced by data-driven decisions. Edward Deming helped American business shift from a top-down model to a bottom-up approach in its thinking about the pursuit of quality and profit. A key ingredient to this change was Deming's principle (1986). That is, real change occurs fastest when the people closest to the problem are working on the solution. The Deming approach is predicated on continuous improvement of work processes, which are the core operating functions of an organization. Deming believed that improving processes is the key to improving quality and that workers want to do their best work. Managers work with employees to gather information and implement process improvement. Instead of blaming individuals for errors, focus is on improving the process that caused the error. Employees are provided with and encouraged to seek training and further education to assist in improving the production system and preventing errors. All leadership, management, and effort are directed toward ensuring quality through continuous improvement.

> **Instead of blaming individuals for errors, focus is on improving the process that caused the error.**

Drucker, a well-respected management expert, supports Deming when he says each employee of a successful company must ask this question: "If you want to know what development I need, ask first, what results are expected of me" (quoted in Deming, 1986). The field of advertising shifted to a market research focus when it discovered how effective it was to follow the numbers. The magic and art of advertising remains, but the industry targets consumers based on what is working—results, not process.

What Deming Says...

Put everyone in the organization to work to accomplish the transformation. The transformation is everybody's job. (1986)

Medicine

The field of medicine is a rich source of experience with data-driven decision making. Medicine was more magic than science. Until the twentieth century, there was no precise testing of any treatment. If the patient didn't die, doctors accepted that whatever treatment had been given must have worked. Until the scientific method was applied to testing treatments, treatment was a hit-or-miss choice.

But, when the scientific method was applied rigorously, medicine advanced. What, exactly, is the scientific method? Simply put, it means that a treatment or a hypothesis is subjected to a rigorous testing to see if the treatment works or the hypothesis is true. It proves the efficacy of the treatment for the problem. Choice becomes more informed, removing its previous hit-or-miss characteristic.

Education, like medicine, benefits from the adoption of proven methods. The NCLB Act of 2001 notes its application to education: scientifically based research "means research that involves the application of rigorous, systematic, and objective procedures to obtain reliable and valid knowledge relevant to education activities and programs" (*NCLB*, 2001).

Education, like medicine, benefits from the adoption of proven methods.

What Medical History Says ...

For decades, doctors have required solid research before treating patients. This scientific approach has produced some of the most effective remedies and the most impressive cures in human history.

Scientific research finds the best way to help those kids who need it most. By using solid research we can get the best ideas to kids who will fail without them. For example, an experiment might involve teaching two groups of children to read using different methods and compare the results to see which method is most successful. Some children will learn to read with a variety of methods. Children having problems learning to read need the most effective methods. Effective teaching and goal-centered curricula can challenge children and interest them in learning — preventing problems of violence, hyperactivity and misidentification of learning disabilities. (www.ed.gov/nclb/)

In the Educational World

Baldrige

"Baldrige is a perfect educational reform model to use with mandated assessments," says Richard J. Noeth, director of American College Test's Office of Policy Research and a co-author of the report, *The Promise of Baldrige in K12 Education.* "Testing provides educators with valuable data on what is and is not working when it comes to children's learning. That information can be used to decide how to distribute resources in such a way that would benefit the entire educational process in a particular school or district" (American College Test, 2003).

The Baldrige Foundation funds and promotes the pursuit of excellence in business and education. The foundation measures areas to determine excellence; one key area is data or information management. In their words, "The Information and Analysis Category examines your organization's information management and performance measurement systems and how your organization analyzes performance data and information" (Baldrige, 2003). The Baldrige criteria were developed originally for the business world in response to concerns about the quality of American manufacturing in the 1970s. Educational strategists and leaders then began to investigate ways in which to apply the quality principles of the model to education. The Baldrige criteria, involving elements such as leadership, strategic planning, focus, analysis of information, and management, were developed and piloted in the 1980s.

What the Baldrige Foundation says ...

What information/data will need to be collected and analyzed before making changes in

programs or student services? How will changes improve student-learning results so they no longer require remediation and the district vision, mission, and strategic goals are met? What are the critical measures of success and how is this data analyzed and used to improve instructional design of programs and courses? (Baldrige, 2003)

Haycock

A look at educational research reveals studies that support data-driven decisions. Haycock, of The Education Trust, has shown that the number one factor in determining the success of a child is teacher quality. Quality teachers are defined as caring, qualified, and working with high expectations toward specific goals that demand rigor from students. *Quality teachers* have a varied and skilled instructional repertoire that they are able to modify as the situation requires, making changes based on results.

What Katie Haycock Says ...

Teachers matter, ... a lot (Haycock, 1999).

Another research discovery is that successful teachers make clear the educational goals of the classroom and share this information with the students. This creates a goal for both parties to the teaching/learning experience.

Reeves

Reeves' research (2003) on the 90-90-90 schools (90% racial minority, 90% lower socioeconomic level, 90% at or above grade level) revealed five common characteristics of these unlikely success stories:

• A focus on academic achievement.

• Clear curriculum choices.

• Frequent assessment of student progress and multiple opportunities for improvement.

■ □ ■ □ ■

• An emphasis on writing.

• External scoring.

The term 90/90/90 was coined by Reeves while doing research in the Milwaukee Public schools between 1995 and 1998. A focus on student achievement meant that he hallways were dripping with reminders of academic goals, results from previous tests, and clear examples of exemplary work completed by the current students. This served as an example and as inspiration. The focus on achievement and clear curriculum choices resulted in an emphasis on the core subjects, reading, mathematics and writing. These areas were targeted in order to improve student opportunities for success in a wide variety of other academic endeavors later.

The focus on achievement and clear curriculum choices resulted in an emphasis on the core subjects, reading, mathematics and writing.

Frequent assessments constructed by classroom teachers resulted in current, reliable data that teachers could use to inform their practice. Multiple opportunities to prove mastery encouraged resiliency and not the discouragement that comes from a single test that reflects a year of learning.

Writing was the most common characteristic of the 90/90/90 schools in the area of performance assessments. The use of written responses appears to help teachers obtain better diagnostic information about students, and certainly helps students demonstrate the thinking process that they employed to find a correct (or even an incorrect) response to an academic challenge.

■ □ ■ □ ■

External scoring was when schools developed common assessment practice and reinforced those common practices through regular exchanges of student papers. This helped the school in its effort to achieve common goals and students were not as likely to suffer arbitrary scoring at the hands of individual teachers.

What Doug Reeves Says...

The significance of the 90/90/90 schools is that they collectively make clear that the demographic characteristics of students do not predict the destiny of those student. (2003)

No Child Left Behind Act of 2001

How relevant is results-oriented decisions to the classroom? With the passage of the No Child Left Behind Act of 2001, funding for schools depends on performance. Under the mandate of this act, the Department of Education disaggregates performance data and determines which schools have shown adequate yearly improvement. To improve intelligently and to produce higher student achievement, schools will need to make decisions based on sound data. The NCLB Act of 2001 describes the key characteristics of reliable research:

Funding for schools depends on performance.

- Scientific Method: A hypothesis about what works or how it works is formulated; a treatment group and control group are used in a study to try to disprove the hypothesis.

- Replicated: Several studies find the same result.

- Generalized: Study findings can be applied broadly to students other than the ones studied.

- Meets Rigorous Standards: The study's design, measures and interpretation of results meet rigorous standards of peer review.

- Convergent findings: Results found from various studies all point to the same conclusion.

The procedure presented in this book is a form of scientific research. It can help teachers create sound data as well as use that data to improve their instructional decisions.

What NCLB Says ...

No Child Left Behind is designed to change the culture of American schools by closing the achievement gap, offering more flexibility, giving parents more options, and teaching students based on what works. (*NCLB*, 2001)

Thanks to scientific research, teachers now know how to teach children to read. Research can help them know how to teach content in other areas in the same way. The No Child Left Behind Act is intended to bring solid, research-based programs to schools throughout the nation.

How to Use This Book

The remaining chapters of this book introduce the data, dialogue, decision process that is based on Schmoker's results-driven model, discuss each of the three parts of the process in detail, introduce four critical questions, and suggest some troubleshooting techniques for frequently encountered implementation problems.

■ □ ■ □ ■

In addition to actually reading the book (!), we suggest enhancing the book's message by using one of the four approaches, discussed next, for interacting with the book's content.

Four-Step Walk-Through

The four-step walk-through method uses cues at the end of each chapter to review the reading and suggest how a teacher can use the material. These cues are the heart of the data, dialogue, decision process. The four questions review the chapter, encourage applying the chapter's material immediately, and reinforce a metacognitive routine for the reader.

Study Group: Read, Then Do

In this approach to working with the book, teachers begin immediately using available data to work with this process for making data-driven decisions. Teachers in the same grade or different grades can use this book as a handbook—a "how-to" guide—to begin the process in their own school on their own time schedule.

Partner: Read And Do

Roger and David Johnson suggest that cooperative groups begin with a two-person group—pairs. A pair of teachers using this process can achieve great things. Although different than a grade-level team, a motivated pair can be effective as it brings the power of the classroom teacher to bear on the problem.

■ ☐ ■ ☐ ■

Workshop Method

Finally, schools can supplement a process already in place and zero in on the dialogue phase or the data phase or the action phase. For schools or districts who are already looking at data for their school improvement plans or for their SMART goals, this approach to using the book can be a perfect complement because it focuses on simplicity and flexibility. Even without the latest or most accurate data, workshops help schools get to work on the data they do have and learn the process of results-driven decisions.

In conclusion, we suggest that you use this book as a guide to help you develop your own data-driven decision-making processes. You may modify this process in your own school among your own peers, but if the results of your own meetings don't proceed as planned, review the book to get back on track. Remember, working with data in a results-driven process is not natural to the schoolhouses that we are all familiar with. Anticipate that there will be stops and starts along the way, but be assured that this is a skill that teachers and staff can master.

Chapter 1
The Data! Dialogue! Decisions! Process

This book addresses a significant fundamental change that teachers are bringing to their classrooms: the concept of results-driven or data-driven instructional decisions in the educational process. Change itself, however, is not a monolithic concept. For most people, change involves at least four components, all of which must change to produce a change in process: knowledge (professional development), belief, student achievement, practice. Which reflects your understanding of how change happens? Gusky presents two views of how change happens, that he calls myth and reality (Figure 1.1). One view, myth, begins with training, which alters belief, which modifies practice, which improves student achievement. On the other hand, reality begins with training, which modifies practice, which improves student achievement, which creates belief. As the Figure 1.1 titles suggest, reality reflects the educational process of engendering change. And, that same reality reflects a results-driven approach to instructional choices.

Change Game	
Myth	**Reality**
Change with professional development	Change with professional development
Change belief	Change practice
Change practice	Change student achievement
Change student achievement	Change belief

Figure 1.1

Schmoker's Model of Results-Driven Change

Schmoker (1996) claims that, for too long, education as a profession has been more driven by process (process driven), adopting or rejecting practices based on leadership, topical movements, or legislated mandates. He advocates creating schools that are driven by results (results driven) instead. As Schmoker implies, teachers working together, with data and with goals, is one of the most powerful ways to change achievement in the classroom.

What Mike Schmoker says ...

Data are to goals what signposts are to travelers; data are not end points, but data are essential to reaching them ... The signposts on the road to school improvement. Thus data and feedback are interchangeable. (1996, p. 30).

The move from the top-down model of management complements Schmoker's assertion that classroom teachers are the most important change agents in results-driven education. He presents a three-part results-driven process (Figure 1.2).

Schmoker's Results-Driven Process

| Managed Data | Meaningful Teamwork | Measurable Goals |

Figure 1.2

■ □ ■ □ ■

Schmoker argues for a broad array of managed data while recognizing that such specific data carries with it a certain risk, and noting the need for personal safety before teachers, individually or in teams, will be willing to take the risk of setting measurable goals (and, in many cases, be the data gatherers). For the best results, the data should not be collected to eliminate poor teachers or create high stakes stress for the students. Well-manage data are collected and analyzed collaboratively and anonymously across department levels and include input from the classroom teachers most affected by the outcomes.

> **Schmoker argues for a broad array of managed data.**

Meaningful teams brainstorm many possible ideas to help break out of old patterns and then create solutions to improve student learning. They add rigor to the process by consistently going back to assess previous goals and judging their success. Structured cooperative strategies help teams accomplish more meaningful work in less time and avoid demoralizing time wasting.

Measurable goals, to be less threatening to the teachers, need to be written simply, based on standards, focused on achievement, and few enough in numbers so teachers concentrate their efforts and create a safe environment. A school that is working toward meaningful change also share the goals in a public place, making the overall success of the school everyone's concern.

Data! Dialogue! Decisions! Model

The Data! Dialogue! Decisions! model is simple and easy to implement. The model grew from 15 yeas of working with teachers and administrators in the analysis of data and is an outgrowth of Schmoker's (1996) data model of managed data, meaningful teams, and measurable goals.

The three-step process provides a cyclic model of data analysis. The cycle begins when participants choose a piece of data that will influence student achievement, continues with dialogue between partners or a team about the data, and ends when participants decide what to implement, quickly, to make "breakthrough" instructional choices. Depending on the results, the cycle starts again by revisiting the initial data set or by choosing a new piece of data to work with.

The Data! Dialogue! Decisions! model is simple and easy to implement.

The next three chapters present each step individually.

Chapter 2
Data!

Data! is the first element of a results-driven process. To start appreciating the value of data, look at Figures 2.1 and 2.2, one of which shows a humorous, questionable use of data whereas the other showcases a serious, exemplary view of data.

WHY AM I SO TIRED?

For a couple years I've been blaming it on lack of sleep, not enough sunshine, too much pressure from my job, earwax buildup, poor blood, or anything else I could think of. But, now I have found the real reason: overwork. Here's why:

The population of this country is 273 million.

There are 140 million retired, which leaves 133 million to do the work.

There are 85 million in school, which leaves 48 million to do the work.

There are 29 million employed by the federal government, leaving 19 million to do the work.

There are 2.8 million in the armed forces, preoccupied with Iraq, which leaves 16.2 million to do the work.

Subtract the 14,800,000 people who work for state and city governments and that leaves 1.4 million to do the work.

At any given time there are 188,000 people in hospitals, leaving 1,212,000 to do the work.

Now, there are 1,211,998 people in prisons.

That leaves just 2 people to do the work.

You and me.

And there you are, sitting here, reading jokes.

Nice, real nice.

Figure 2.1

Stand and Deliver (Jaime Escalante: Math Teacher-AP Calculus Exam)

1982, 18 of his students passed the exam

1983, 30 of his students passed the exam

1984, 63 of his students passed the exam

1985, 77 of his students passed the exam

1986, 78 of his students passed the exam

1987, 87 of his students passed the exam

(From Menéndez, R. (Director), *Stand and Deliver* [Motion picture], 1988)

Figure 2.2

Isn't data fun? Or is it? Use Figure 2.3 to gauge your view of data.

Data! Data! Data!

Do you agree or disagree with the following statements:

1. Data is/are plural.

2. Data reveal patterns, trends and gaps.

3. I have not been on a data in a long time.

4. Data represented in graphs make the information easily accessible.

5. To disaggregate data, **aggravates** some.

6. Data-driven decisions, through data dialogues, get results.

7. To manage data, rank these steps by importance:

   ____ Gather   ____ Analyze   ____ Interpret

8. I say tomato, not tomato? I say data, not data?

9. **Hard** data is more reliable and more valid than **soft** data.

10. Technology helps to manage information/data.

Figure 2.3

For Schmoker, "Data almost always point to action— they are the enemy of comfortable routines. By ignoring data, we promote inaction and inefficiency" (Schmoker, 1999a, p. 39).

A Sign of the Times

Since the 1990s, educators have developed a considerably stronger habit of collecting data to make decisions. Several factors have pushed this movement to the forefront of education. Legislation, specifically the No Child Left Behind

Act of 2001 (NCLB), has pressed educators to examine different types of data. NCLB says that no child may be left behind [a grade in school] based on academic performance on yearly standardized or state assessments. The test scores must be disaggregated to reveal subgroups—such as those based on ethnicity or income—of students' scores.

An additional factor in the movement toward data is the vast improvement of data collection methods.

Technology allows educators to collect an array of data.

Technology allows educators to collect an array of data and to view that data for individual students, classrooms, grade levels, schools, and districts. Using the Internet, educators can view data in real time. With the technology, educators easily collect student subgroup data as required by NCLB.

Of course, some educators are more comfortable with technological input to their teaching than other educators. Figure 2.4 identifies five levels of comfort; readers might want to locate theirs, for future planning.

■ □ ■ □ ■

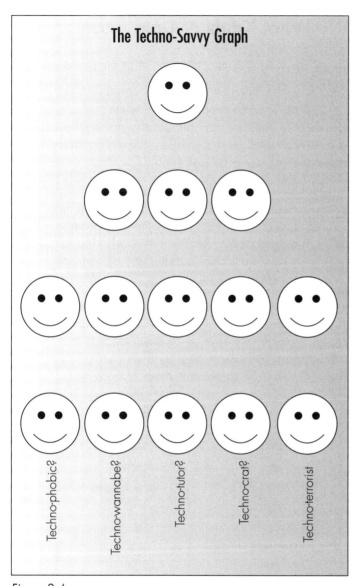

Figure 2.4

What Kinds of Data Exist?

Data can be characterized as quantitative or qualitative—hard or soft data.

Quantitative data represent information that can be measured. Quantitative data are used in statistical analysis and in the compilation, presentation, discussion, and interpretation of numerical data.

Hard data are statistical and numeric. Soft data are subjective.

Qualitative data refer to detailed narrative descriptions and explanations of phenomena investigated, with lesser emphasis given to numerical qualifications. Methods used to collect qualitative data include ethnographic practices such as observing and interviewing.

Hard data are statistical and numeric. Soft data are subjective. Both types of data may be analyzed, and both types have proven to be effective. Both can be life changing when manipulated by a systemic analysis process. Figure 2.5 lists characteristics of each type.

Two Types of Data

Quantitative	Qualitative
Objective	Descriptive
Statistics	Anecdotal Reports
Standardized Tests	Informal
Textbook Tests	Subjective
Numerical	Projects
Calculations	Dialogue

Figure 2.5

What Kinds of Data Are Available?

School district administrators receive large amounts of data on a consistent basis. With the technology that is available to schools, all types of data could be fruitfully collected, streamlined, and analyzed. Different types of data are used at different levels within the education hierarchy. Two major sources of data include student assessment data and demographic data.

Two major sources of data include student assessment data and demographic data.

Student Assessment Data

1. *Standardized assessments.* The standardized assessments are norm-referenced tests (see Figure 2.6 for definition), giving stakeholders a comparison to other students, schools, and districts within the United States. Norm-referenced tests report results against a norm or average. These assessments also provide critical data on trends within classrooms and across buildings.

2. *State assessments.* Ideally, a state assessment is aligned to the content standards adopted by the state. These assessments may provide criterion-referenced (see Figure 2.6 for definition), norm-referenced information, or a combination of both. They are often high-stakes tests, with results published in local newspapers.

3. *Benchmark assessments.* School districts are starting to implement assessments developed locally and aligned to the state and national assessments. Benchmark assessments are administered several times throughout the year, within the same time period for all students. These benchmark assessments should give teachers some

predictive information regarding how the students will score on the standardized or state assessments.

4. *Classroom assessments.* Classroom assessments may include teacher-made tests, rubrics, observations, work samples, and/or student portfolios. The challenge for teachers is to ensure these types of assessments align to state standards.

Demographic Data

1. *Student demographics.* Types of student demographic data include ethnicity, socioeconomic levels, special needs, attendance, gender, discipline records, and so forth (Bernhardt, 2003, p. 29).

2. *Staff demographics.* Staff demographics data include teacher-student ratio, teacher strengths, and types of certifications (Bernhardt, 2003, p. 29).

3. *School demographics.* The school safety and crime data along with the different types of extracurricular activities being implemented may provide insight to an array of available resources and/or gaps in resources (Bernhardt, 2003, p. 29).

4. *Community demographics.* Types of data to be collected regarding the community include makeup of the population, economic base, community/business involvement, or support agencies (Bernhardt, 2003, p. 29).

Norm-Referenced versus Criterion-Referenced Tests

"What is the difference between norm-referenced and criterion-referenced tests?"

Criterion-referenced testing or content-referenced testing compares the test taker's performance to a performance standard or to the degree of mastery in a defined domain.

Norm-referenced testing compares the test taker's performance to the performance of other test takers.

Figure 2.6

While working with a team of teachers from the Chicago Public schools, a teacher noted, "I didn't realize we had so much data to analyze." If there are no data, then they should be created, and there should be no excuses. When the data piece to be analyzed is determined, it is important to trust the data. "No assessment is perfect, but the analysis of the results can provide life changing information" Schmoker (2000, p. 62).

> **When the data piece to be analyzed is determined, it is important to trust the data.**

Determining where there is a critical need within a school assists the educators in choosing the type of data to analyze. Figure 2.7 gives several examples of the types of data that are available in many schools. Marking, although schools vary greatly in the accuracy and amount of data they collect. When teachers first look at the data situation for their schools, the list in Figure 2.7 (mark + for the most used and – for the least used) can be a good beginning.

■□■□■

Existing Data in Schools

Mark Most Used (+) or Least Used (-)

School Data

1. Student Grades
2. Absentee Rates
3. eferrals
4. Detentions
5. College Admissions
6. Scholarships
7. Qualified Teacher
8. Teacher Attendance

Testing

9. Norm-Referenced Tests
10. Criterion Referenced Tests
11. Scholastic Aptitude Tests
12. Foreign Language Proficiency Tests
13. Vocational Aptitude Tests

Observations

14. Student Work Habits
15. Group Interactions
16. Physical Education Skills
17. Social Skills
18. Study Habits
19. Motivation

Student Work Samples

20. Writing
21. Reading
22. Math Problem Solving
23. Art Work
24. Group Projects
25. Performance Videos
26. Portfolios
27. Electronic Portfolios

Surveys/Questionnaires

28. Students
29. Parents
30. Communities
31. Teachers
32. Administrators

Teacher Work Samples

33. Teacher-Made Tests
34. Homework Assignments
35. Rubrics
34. Project Assignments
36. Performances
37. Videotaped Lessons
38. Peer Observations Checklist
39. Action Research
40. Professional Development Experiences

Figure 2.7

How Are Data Collected?

There are a variety of data collection methods available to schools, but they fall into these two main categories: traditional and technology-enhanced. Figure 2.8 gives a brief overview of each type.

Comparison of Traditional and Technology-Enhanced Data Collection

Traditional	Technology-Enhanced
File folders	On-line access
The Green Grade Book	Databases
Paper grade books	Integrated systems
Typewriter	(Student information with report cards)
Carbon copy report cards	
Three-ring binders of curriculum	Easily accessible
	Enter once and many users access
Hand written notes to parents	On-line testing
Scan cards	E-mail

Figure 2.8

Traditional Collection

The traditional method of collection is a manual paper-and-pencil method. Continuous collection of data using the traditional method varies from school to school, depending on funding for technology. If schools are currently collecting data using traditional methods and are getting results, the process being implemented works. Although collecting data in file folders is becoming an outdated method, traditional methods of collecting data do have their place. Even when data are collected manually, the three-phase process of Data! Dialogue! Decisions! can be implemented by the collectors. Whether using a traditional method of data collection or technology, ask the following questions to determine if the results are what you want:

Are we improving student achievement?

Are we able to access the data in a timely manner?

Are the data relevant?

Are the data accurate?

Are the data continuous?

Using Technology to Collect Data

Advances in technology allow users to collect different types of data.

Advances in technology allow users to collect different types of data in formats that are easily accessible and user friendly. *Instructional management systems* allow users to collect student academic performance data related to the curriculum. These systems provide schools a way to enter the district's curriculum outline, to complete lesson plans, to align relevant content, and to assess the students based on the curriculum. Instructional management systems also allow users to view students' local and standardized assessment data by individual student, class, building, or district as it relates to their district's curriculum. Instructional management systems provide critical information centered on instruction individualized to the needs of the students. Having a connection between the day-to-day instruction and standardized, state or locally developed assessments is a key component of an instructional management system.

Discipline systems allow users to collect and track the discipline records of students. These systems provide discipline reports of students related to the number of incidents, time frame, severity, and consequences of the related behavior.

Reporting systems related to standardized tests allow users to view the results based on the tested statements. Districts have the ability to compare their student population to other districts.

Figure 2.8 outlines the differences between traditional methods of data collection and current methods.

How Are the Data Used?

Data can bring about change in the educational process through school implementations, by using high stakes data, and by increasing student achievement. These are just different ways of accommodating what Joyce, Wolf, and Calhoun highlight (quoted in Schmoker, 1996, p. 17): "We did not find a single case in the literature where student learning increased but had not been a central goal."

■□■□■

School Implementations

Assessment Data for Grades

> **Collecting data linked to student performance on specific standards allows teachers to use a variety of teaching strategies/techniques to support students in their learning.**

Teachers daily collect data on student performance, both formally and informally. Collecting data linked to student performance on specific standards allows teachers to use a variety of teaching strategies/techniques to support students in their learning. For example, after teaching a lesson, a teacher may ask the students for a "Thumbs Up" if they understood the concept, thus collecting informal information on how the class is doing. A more formal collection might include rubric data on student performance, which, as part of the teacher's grade book, becomes part of the students' final grades.

Assessment Data for Grouping

Knowing how many students are meeting or not meeting a particular standard gives teachers information needed to target specific subgroup shortfalls within the classroom. With on-going collection of student data related to standards, teachers can consistently group and re-group students based on what the data show.

Assessment Data for Policy Setting

Administration in a suburban middle school in Illinois determined that there was in increase of students being sent to the office for discipline issues. The administration decided to collect data centered on the number of students that were being sent to the office, during what time period, what teacher was sending the students, and the severity of the offence. The data collected were both quantitative and qualitative. Figure 2.9 is a sample of the collected data.

Discipline Data Collection Example

Time of Discipline Issue	Grade Level	Student Name	Room Number	Discipline Issue
Before School (7:30am)	6	Kacey Jones	303	Hitting another student
After School (2:30pm)	6	Mike Macy	205	Throwing food
5th Period Math	6	Kerry Kinney	102	Talking

Figure 2.9

The data were collected daily and reviewed weekly. When analyzing the data, teachers recognized a pattern—the majority of incidents occurred before and after school. Based on the pattern they found, the staff knew where to concentrate their attention.

Collecting relevant data assists in confirming relevant predictions regarding the educational process. Initially, the staff met in grade-level teams to analyze the data. This gave them a clear picture about what was happening at their grade level.

Vertical Team

Vertical teaming is another meeting strategy that assists in the analysis of the data and the communication process within the school. Understanding what the issues are in other grade levels and how they are being addressed gives teachers a broader perspective of the school and district. Vertical teaming can be implemented by clustering grade levels, for example, K-2, 2-4, or by meeting with the grades above and below one grade level.

> **Vertical teaming is another meeting strategy that assists in the analysis of the data and the communication process within the school.**

High Stakes Data

High stakes data get their name because the data are used to make choices that have large impacts on students, teachers, administrators, and school districts. And, high stakes data are usually published locally. When published, the overall school scores typically are ranked according to performance—highest to lowest. Publishing of these scores not only affects the members of the school but also the community at large. For example, the purchase of homes may depend on the performance of the school that serves that neighborhood.

Teacher or Student Actions

High stakes data have been used to choose whether to retain or release students, to pen or close schools, or to hire or fire teachers and administrators. Many administrators' and teachers' contracts are linked to student achievement on high stakes assessments. There have been many debates about using standardized testing data in actions that have students or staff consequences. Amrein and Berliner report, "Currently, eighteen states use

> **Many administrators' and teachers' contracts are linked to student achievement on high stakes assessments.**

assessment data to grant or withhold diplomas: Alabama, Florida, Georgia, Indiana, Louisiana, Maryland, Minnesota, Mississippi, Nevada, New Jersey, North Carolina, Ohio, South Carolina, Tennessee, Texas, and Virginia. Most of these states also attach their state assessment to a broad range of consequences such as identifying low performing schools, publish school report cards, grade to grade promotion and /or graduation contingent on high school graduation exam" (2003, p. 32).

Parent Choice and Use of Vouchers

The NCLB has given parents' the option of choosing a school because of the discontinuity between the desire for improved student performance and reality of continued low student performance. Based on performance ratings using the high stakes data, when a school is under-performing or is unsafe for a specified amount of time, parents may opt to transfer their child to a high performing school.

Parents may opt to transfer their child to a high performing school.

Districts have responded to these empowering uses of high stakes data by setting policies to analyze student performance using high stakes data as one factor and attendance, grades, and locally developed assessments as other factors. Even with the emphasis on high stakes assessments, a 1999 study showed that fewer than one half the states in the United States require competence in assessments for licensure as a teacher (Guskey, 2003).

■ □ ■ □ ■

Data for Increased Student Achievement

Deciding What Data to Use

When choosing data, choose data that are relevant, meaningful, easily accessible, capable of impacting student achievement, and collected on an on-going basis. "The data must be used judiciously and with discretion" (Peters, quoted in Schmoker, 1996, p. 29).

For example, when a team decides to analyze the results of the standardized assessments, they do so at one period in time. The assessment is given yearly, and in almost all cases, the data are returned to the school at the end of the school year. The analysis of this high stakes assessment data is a starting place for school districts. Although this is good starting place, a continuous process of tracking student growth during the year is needed to make decisions regarding the data and to increase student achievement.

When determining which data to use in the Data! Dialogue! Decisions! process, consider the questions in Figure 2.10.

Determining What Data to Use

Where are the concerns already?
This could be low student attendance, low scores on the high stakes assessment, an higher number of discipline referrals, a rise in the number of students not meeting state standards in mathematics, or more students not meeting expectations on the local assessments in reading comprehension.

■ □ ■ □ ■

What data strike you as most significant?

Significant data may be a dramatic change from year to year resulting in an increase or decrease in scores. Determining a data piece that has had positive results facilitates positive change.

What data provide an opportunity for rapid results?

Determine priority areas that, when focused on, improve overall performance within the standard/subject area or across other disciplines. For example, if the majority of students are not meeting expectations on "reading comprehension: drawing conclusions," focus on that topic because the students are more likely to perform better on other skills areas within reading comprehension and in social studies, etc. when this area is attended to.

Figure 2.10

Let Data Inform Practice

To achieve the best results with data, educators need to install a process that involves all staff in collecting, analyzing, and applying the lessons learned from the data. Create teams, and insure that each staff member is involved with at least one team. Actively create opportunities to collect and use data. Collections created consistently, periodically, and over time are invaluable resources for decision making, assessment, and comparison with previous achievements. Figure 2.11 shows a few means of making the best use of data. This is a continuous process allowing data to inform practice.

Actively create opportunities to collect and use data.

■☐■☐■

How Best to Use Data

Put a process in place

Train staff members to work in data teams

Use data consistently, periodically, continuously

Figure 2.11

Chapter 3
Dialogue!

The second part of the Data! Dialogue! Decisions! process is dialogue. To make the best use of data in consistent and systemic ways, teachers need to build a process that addresses how often and what types of data will be reviewed. Each staff member is assigned to a data team that consistently analyzes pieces of data. By consistently reviewing the data, team members begin to inform their practices. The data teams write their findings in common locations so both process and results are available for all to view.

> **By consistently reviewing the data, team members begin to inform their practices.**

Teaming to Ask and Answer
the Questions

Teaming is one way to decide what data a school or group of teachers want to work with.

It has been said many times that the teaching staff in a school is just like a classroom of students. There are the informal leaders, the come along, the people pleasers, the cut-ups, and the disinterested observers. When challenged to set up teams to look at data and make instructional decisions, teachers always come back to what works—the classic cooperative structures.

> **Teachers always come back to what works—the classic cooperative structures.**

Johnson, Johnson, and Holubec (1986) say that a good cooperative group has interdependence, studies together but tests alone, finds strength in the diversity of the members, and is stronger the more diverse the group members are. A common feature of cooperative groups is a series of roles that provide structure, help expand talents, enrich discussions, and engage participants with challenge.

In the beginning, to help groups become high-functioning teams, teams should adopt fundamental aspects of cooperative learning. For example, a leader should be picked randomly and leadership should rotate each time the group meets. To prevent one teacher from dominating the discussion when looking at the data, each teacher takes a turn at remarking on what takes their attention or what they see in the data.

Be aware that some staff members are very comfortable in their roles in the school and because of this, may be reluctant to break character. But, by structuring the interactions, teachers have opportunities to grow and change, and, in turn, their practice changes and grows.

Other issues that come up in teacher teams are emotional issues. Teachers are not used to being the prime decision maker in a public forum. They are confident and assured In the classroom, but they may step back and wait for someone else to make a decision when they are among peers. Many times they wait for directions from authority higher in the school structure. A technique to help teachers feel empowered is to have them add up all of the years of education that they have on their team and then divide by the number of teachers on the team.

■ □ ■ □ ■

The Four Questions in Brief

Figure 3.1 graphically introduces four questions that constitute the process that teams use as they look at the data.

Four Questions

Question	Explanation
What? DATA!	What data do we have?
What Else? DIALOGUE!	What else do we know or need to know?
So, What? DIALOGUE!	So, what inferences can we make?
Now, What? DECISION!	Now, what instructional interventions will get results; Professional Development? What is your action plan? Who will do what when?

Figure 3.1

First, **What** did you find? The response to this question describes the existing data in some detail, connects to previous data or to an existing concern, and requires observation and as good a description as can be developed at first glance.

Second, **What else** do you *know or need to know*? Here, team members look for additional information about the situation in order to describe and analyze the data more thoroughly. They identify supporting evidence and/or conflicting evidence (but trust the existing data and work with it).

Third, **So, what** does the data say? Team members discuss the data collaboratively, as a team of experts. They may use large charts for recording data so that they may all view it together. Teams avoid finger-pointing by disguising the names and classrooms represented in the data. They approach the data as a problem-solving scenario, and put their heads together to seek meaningful inferences and logical conclusions.

Fourth, **Now, what** do you need to do? What will change? What is implied? What is indicated by the data? What instructional goal(s) might be set? How might the team use the data to increase student achievement? What support do teachers need in terms of professional development to do what needs to be done?

`The dialogue revolves around these four questions and focuses on problem solving for results. By using these four questions in a professional dialogue, the tendencies for finger-pointing or playing the "blame game" are sidestepped.

The Four Questions in Full

Figure 3.2 shows the four questions visually. As the Data! Dialogue! Decisions! process is discussed next, let's follow a team that chose to address the problem of 4,000 disciplinary referrals in a year in their school to demonstrate the type of responses that these questions might have (Figures 3.3 through 3.6).

■□■□■

The Four Questions

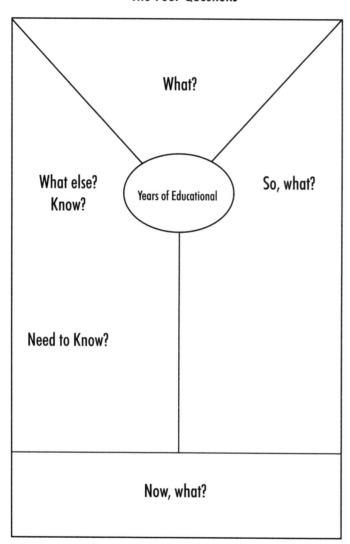

Figure 3.2

WHAT?

The importance of establishing the "What?" is clearly illustrated in this simple joke:

Two men are attempting to move a very big piano on a very steep, very narrow stairwell on a very hot day. They are sweating, grunting and groaning, working very hard.

Finally, one man says, "We will never get this thing up these stairs."

The other man says, "Up? I thought we taking it down."

The "What?" question needs to be specific and not too broad. For example, teachers looking at test results might say, "The 'What?' is reading scores. We will work on improving the reading scores." Although this sounds admirable, it becomes clear later that this is too vague of a definition of the data. A better response to looking at the test results might be, "The 'What?' is understand the big idea. We will look at ways to improve test scores in the area of understanding the big idea."

As teachers become comfortable with examining data, they learn to focus on specific areas.

When first beginning to look at data, data can be intimidating. As teachers become comfortable with examining data, they learn to focus on specific areas.

One thing to remember about the "What?" is that, when teachers are committed to working with data to improve instruction, they know they will be returning to the results over and over again through the year and through their careers. Too much time spent deciding on the "What?" can be discouraging and counterproductive. Keep the process of choosing the target data simple. Figure 3.3 shows the chart from the discipline example.

What Data?
What Data ... do we have?
Situation: Middle School; 600 students in Grades 6 to 8;
Data   Problem: 4,000 disciplinary referrals in 2002

Figure 3.3

WHAT ELSE?

After choosing the data to work with, teams ask themselves "What else?" do they know? It is here that the power of teachers working together on their own data really takes root. Teachers know so much more than the data show on the statistical print out, and here is where they can offer this knowledge. The "What?" may be hard data (the stuff on the statistical print out) but the "What else?" could be soft data (facts that seasoned staff know about a problem that may not be evident on first glance).

"What else?" is the question that gets teachers conversing about solving the problem. This question helps them focus on the specific and draw conclusions based on what they know about the data. For example, a team of teachers close to the situation might know how a re-districting plan has affected the student population, a fact not reflected in the test results. Figure 3.4 shows the "What else?" sheet from the discipline example.

What Else?		
	What Else ... do we know?	**What Else ... do we need to know?**
Dialogue	-increase of 20% from 2001	-Who? Students? Teachers?
	-new principal	-When? Hrs? Days? Wks? Months?
	-new zoning /district boundaries	-Where? Locations
	-"study hall atmosphere"	-Consequences?

Figure 3.4

SO, WHAT?

A third question that is particularly useful in the Dialogue! stage is "So, What?" Now, teachers connect the dots and make some statements that may not be reported on the page but are, instead, inferences or logical conclusions. The "So, what?" brings out gaps, overlaps, and trends. It becomes clear to many teachers, for the first time, what has really been happening in their school. They discover the weaknesses in the curriculum or the difference between what they know to be true from their own student observations and what is true as represented by the data.

When a teacher team reaches the "So, What?" stage, they tend to really understand the power of working together as the collective knowledge of the group is evident. It is here that the years of classroom experience become a factor as teachers read between the lines to see the real story. Figure 3.5 shows the "So, What?" chart from one group in one workshop.

So, What?		
	So, What … does an analysis reveal?	*So, What* … can we infer?
Dialogue	-re-zoning add 168 Hispanic from apartment complex -65% referrals from 5 teachers	-Detention is not a *real* consequence -some teachers interpret differently; some not using referral strategy; consequences not enough

Figure 3.5

NOW, WHAT?

Before addressing the fourth question, teams may want to shore up their confidence. It may come as a surprise to learn how many years of experience are represented on a team, so collect that particular datum by totaling the number of years of experience in education for the team members. Not a small number, right?

"Now, what?" is the question that leads teams to set SMART goals. These goals are the end result of collecting, analyzing, and cooperatively choosing data of interest. They guide change because they represent the desired result of change.

A SMART goal is specific, measurable, achievable, reasonable, and timely. For example, "By the end of the next grading period (6 weeks) reading comprehension, in the learning standards involving theme, character and big idea, will improve from 45% of students meet standards to 85% meets standards." Figure 3.6 shows a few examples of goals worked out by the team addressing a disciplinary problem.

Now, What?		
	Now, What ...	Now, What ...
Decisions	**instruction will work?** -use detention time for additional instruction ...literacy and math **What.... is the target goal?** -Reduce referrals each quarter by 25%	**Professional Development supports the instruction?** -Discipline Strategies Literacy Across Content **Who...will do what?** -Staff Development Team will arrange for in-services for discipline and reading across content

Figure 3.6

Action Plans

An area in which goals are fundamental is in creating and using action plans. Action plans comprise the decisions that teams make to answer the "Who does what when?" question. Specifically, three questions form the basis of the goals in this stage of the Data! Dialogue! Decisions! process:

1. Who will do what?

2. What exactly will they do? And how are they held accountable?

3. When will they do it?

The action plan is directly linked with the SMART goal. Answering the three questions puts the SMART goal into action. Each of the participants determines how the goal will be implemented and how they will be accountable. The accountability factor may be as simple and meaningful as setting the next meeting date to determine progress toward the goal.

Conclusion

A model on large paper can be posted in the teachers' lounge to illustrate a folksy example of the Four Question Process (see Figure 3.7 or consider using Figure 3.8 for team responses). By using this paper example as a standard model, teacher teams share, in a very simple way, what they are doing. Teams also can observe how other teachers' teams, during their Dialogue! stage, answered the questions, What? What, else? So,what? and Now, what?

■□■□■

Posters for the Four Questions

DATA. WHAT?

DIALOGUE. WHAT ELSE? SO WHAT?

DECISIONS NOW, WHAT?

ACTION PLAN WHO WILL DO WHAT WHEN?

Figure 3.7

Data! Dialogue! Decisions!		
	What Data ... do we have?	
Data		
Dialogue	**What Else** ... do we know? (Describe)	**What else** ... do we need to know? (Describe)
Dialogue	**So, What** ... does an analysis reveal?	**So, What** ... can we infer?
Decisions	**Now, What** ... instruction will work?	**Now, What** ... Professional Development supports this instruction?
Decisions	**What** ... is the target goal?	**Who** ... will do what?

Figure 3.8

The Coaches' Meeting Revisited

Let's revisit the conversation between the coaches, which appeared as a vignette in the preface. This time, notice how the meeting, split into four sections, reflects the four key Dialogue! questions.

Part One: What?

VARSITY COACH. I have been looking over the stats for this year and comparing them to last year. You know what I see?

ASSISTANT COACH. We were better last year.

VARSITY COACH. Yes, but do you know why?

ASSISTANT COACH. We won more games last year.

VARSITY COACH. Brilliant observation ... I know we won more games last year but I noticed something else in the statistics. Something besides wins and losses.

FRESHMAN COACH. I think what you mean is rebounding. We out rebounded the other team in every game we won.

VARSITY COACH. Exactly, rebounding. This year we are not rebounding. Get rebounds and you get the wins, it's that simple. **The "WHAT" is rebounding.**

Part Two: What Else?

ASSISTANT COACH. We had taller players last year. Rebounds come off the rim, the rim is high, tall players have an advantage. Tall players make better rebounders. You tell me how to get kids to grow and our rebounding will improve. When our rebounding improves we'll win more games.

FRESHMAN COACH. But, if you look deeper into the statistics you will see that our big guys always rebounded about equal to the other teams big guys. It was our guards who got the rebounds in the victories. The short quick players get the rebounds that matter.

ASSISTANT COACH. I'd like to see who got the rebounds in the losses, and I would also like to see how other teams rebounded against us versus how they rebounded against other people.

FRESHMAN COACH. OK, sure, and then I could go back a couple years and compare those numbers to the numbers of the best teams in the state by running a analysis on a spreadsheet program on my computer. **The WHAT ELSE is who did the rebounding.**

Part Three: So, What?

VARSITY COACH. Now wait a minute. We want to improve our win loss record. I don't think we have to crunch numbers like Price Waterhouse to do that. I have been coaching for 18 years, you about 13, and you 10. If between us we can't figure out how to improve out team we are in sorry shape.

ASSISTANT COACH. What do you mean, Coach?

VARSITY COACH. Let's look at the numbers that tell us when we rebounding well and when we didn't. Let's look over our practice schedule and see when we worked on rebounding. If we do not emphasis rebounding in practice how do we expect the kids to do it during the game. **The SO, WHAT is the correlation between practice and good rebounding.**

Part Four: Now, What?

FRESHMAN COACH. I got a great drill to teach technique and the kids can do the drill on their own.

ASSISTANT COACH. I think if we tell the kids what we want them to do, really make it clear why it is important to the team.

Instructional Decisions

VARSITY COACH. Until they understand let's have them set some goals. Every kid has to get five rebounds a game.

ASSISTANT COACH. In the next game?

VARSITY COACH. OK, maybe too much too soon. How about three games from now every kid will get at least five rebounds a game and we as a team will out rebound every opponent the rest of the season.

Measurable Achievable Goals

FRESHMAN COACH. Well, we said rebounding leads to victories and so this seems like a plan.

ASSISTANT COACH. If it doesn't get the results we want, then we'll try something else. **The NOW, WHAT included choices about instruction and goals.**

Keep in mind that teachers engaged in a data dialogue will sound very much like the fictional coaches. Keeping an eye on the results, the wins and losses, the individual statistics is easy for sports people, and so it has to in the classroom. It is by paying attention to what is working and repeating these best practices that teachers begin to see a change in the efforts to close the achievement gap.

Chapter 4
Decisions!

The final, critical, and perhaps most difficult step in the Data! Dialogue! Decisions! process is making a decision regarding the data. It is in this stage that questions are asked about goals and actions, for example, What should change? What is implied? What is indicated by the data? What instructional goal(s) might be set? How might the data be used to increase student achievement? What support do teachers need in terms of professional development to do what needs to be done?

SMART Goals

One way to create appropriate goals is to use the acronym SMART to form and assess each goal:

Specific

Measurable

Attainable

Results-oriented

Time Bound

An example of a SMART goal is: Increase students reading comprehension level by 20% in the first quarter by implementing the gap strategies. The goal outlines a specific attainable target area (i.e., reading comprehension), identifies what needs to be done (i.e., implementing the gap strategies) in order to achieve

■□■□■

measurable results (i.e., 20% increase), and sets a deadline (i.e., first quarter).

SMART goals are fundamental to instructional decisions and action plans. Writing SMART goals helps make goals and objectives specific and makes it easier for teams to choose their target data effectively. When writing goals, teams are not merely talking and analyzing the data, they also are developing an action plan to be implemented.

Writing SMART goals helps make goals and objectives specific.

Instructional Decisions

Instructional decisions are the most frequent decisions that teams and teachers make. Teachers live with their instructional decisions in real-time and usually have to adjust their choices on the fly. Thus, a well-constructed SMART goal is crucial when choosing instructional techniques.

One important ingredient of a SMART goal is its teaching strategy, that is, what instructional method will be used? In the example goal at the beginning of this section, that strategy was identified in the by phrase: "by implementing the gap strategies." There are a series of breakthrough strategies that are appropriate for the content of the "by" phrase because they are linked specifically to SMART goals. These include strategies to close the achievement gap, strategies for literacy, strategies based on the best practices of good teachers, and strategies for taking tests.

■ □ ■ □ ■

1. Equitable Distribution of Response Opportunity

2. Affirmation or Correction

3. Proximity

4. Individual Helping

5. Praise for the Learning Performance

6. Courtesy

7. Latency

8. Reasons for Praise

9. Personal Interest Statements and Compliments

10. Delving, Rephrasing, Giving Clues

11. Listening

12. Touching

13. Higher-Level Questioning

14. Accepting Feelings

15. Desisting

Figure 4.1 TESA: Teacher Expectations, Student Achievement

Fogarty's Literacy Matters Strategies

In addition, Fogarty (2001b) suggests an acronym that presents strategies that help teachers foster literacy in the classroom. Figure 4.2 shows this acronym.

Fogarty's Literary Matters Strategies

Learning to learn – *metacognition*

Inquiring readers- *visualize, infer*

Tapping into prior knowledge- *predict*

Extensive reading- *fiction/non-fiction*

Research on the brain- *prior knowledge*

Analysis of words- *word attack skills*

Cooperative learning- *cognitive rehearsal*

You-are-a—reader attitude- *data/feedback*

Mediate with interventions-do *differently*

Appeal to parents-*homework/reading*

Teach vocabulary-*word boxes; booklets*

Technology impacts literacy-*online reading*

Entry points honor multiple intelligences-*eight*

Read aloud, along, appropriately-*every day*

Strategic reading is guided-*DRTA/SQ3R*

Figure 4.2

Nine Best Practices

A third set of strategies is based on Marzano, Pickering, and Pollack's (2001) research. Fogarty and Pete (2003) identify 20 strategies that supported the nine families of classroom instruction that Marzano et al. had found to be the most effective in helping teachers help students learn. Figure 4.3 shows the nine families and the 20 strategies.

Nine Best Practices

FAMILY 1SD: IDENTIFYING SIMILARITIES AND DIFFERENCES
  (compare/contrast; classify; metaphor, analogy)

FAMILY 2SN: SUMMARIZING AND NOTE TAKING
  (delete, substitute, keep; reciprocal teaching; summary frames; outlines; webbing)

FAMILY 3RR: REINFORCING EFFORT AND PROVIDING RECOGNITION
  (Effort rubric; effective praise, pause, prompt, praise; concrete symbols)

FAMILY 4HP: HOMEWORK AND PRACTICE
  (homework policy; focused practice)

FAMILY 5NR: NONLINGUISTIC REPRESENTATIONS
  (graphic representations; models; mental pictures, drawing, kinesthetic activities)

FAMILY 6CL: COOPERATIVE LEARNING
  (2-4…small, heterogeneous groups; informal - formal ,base groups)

FAMILY 7OF: SETTING OBJECTIVES AND PROVIDING FEEDBACK
  (specific, but flexible goals ; contracts); timely, specific feedback)

FAMILY 8GH: GENERATING AND TESTING HYPOTHESES
  (problem solving; decision making, investigations; invention, inquiry)

FAMILY 9QCA: QUESTIONS, CUES, AND ADVANCE ORGANIZERS
  (HOT questions; wait time; pre-learning; cues for inferences; narrative, skimming; graphics as advanced organize)

Figure 4.3

Test Taking Strategies

A fourth set of strategies suggests techniques students can use when taking tests. Again, acronyms concisely identify

important elements of test-taking strategies. There are four:
ESSAY EXAM (Figure 4.4), BE A MATH WIZ (Figure 4.5),
TEST TAKER (for multiple choice questions; Figure 4.6),
and I CAN DO THIS (unpacking the language in test
directions; Figure 4.7). Teachers may use these strategies
in the classroom to help students prepare for tests.

ESSAY EXAM

Examine directions carefully; figure out what is required; answer the question that is asked; use the questions in wording your answer.

Survey all questions before answering any of them; get the lay of the land; see if subsequent questions contain useful information.

Select a title; get a focus; use a metaphor or simile to find similarities; use a magnet word to gather the main ideas and provide a target for your response.

Always outline or use a graphic organizer; get your initial ideas down on paper in a brief graphic format; use these as prewriting tools.

Yes! Read over what you have written! Read each question and each response. Be sure you have answered the question, that it is complete, and that it makes sense; then, read over the entire test.

Elaborate; write long rather than short; give examples to illustrate your ideas; enhance the general statements with relevant details.

X exit with an ending; bring the response to closure; wrap it up with a logical conclusion.

Add evidence to each general statement; cite authorities, whenever possible; give a resource title if you can.

Manage your time: budget it; be aware of the clock and work as fast as you can; don't spend too much time on one questions; pace yourself; you can always go back if your have time.

MATH STRATEGIES

Be sure to use all necessary information; find all relevant facts; use the most "telling" information.

Eliminate unnecessary facts; discard superfluous information; omit anything that seems unnecessary to the question asked.

Attack the test with a positive attitude; be confident of your ability to think and reason; proceed briskly, with affirmations of your skills.

Make educated guesses; use your intuition; let your innate knowledge and understanding guide your process to a solution.

Always estimate before you look at the answers; decide what seems like a reasonable number; what seems logical.

Take the "givens" first; find the "knowns," and then proceed through the problem to the "unknowns"; what do they tell you?

Have a way to check your answers; work it backwards; round it off; try it out in a practical application story.

Work systematically; organize your work; go step by step; don't skip around; be thorough.

Inspect the graphs, charts, and tables carefully; see how they relate to the question; use this displayed information.

Zee the patterns and trends; look for commonalities; look for the themes ad threads that seem to run through the test section.

Figure 4.4

MULTIPLE CHOICE

Time counts! Work quickly and carefully; pace yourself; block out sections and keep on going, no matter what.

Eliminate unlikely answers; find the ones that are clearly wrong; eliminate the obvious ones; sharpen your chances for guessing right.

Scout clues; look for cueing words and/or necessary numbers; find the relevant information; the keys to answering the questions.

Take a guess before you choose; use your intuition; trust your first thought and the connection you are naturally seeing.

Try to give the answers "they" want; give the standard answer; decide what is being tested and give the answer that is most logical.

Always choose the "closest" answer; don't get creative; go with the probable response over the possible response.

Keep going! Never give up! You will pick up points as you go through the test systematically; trust the percentages; do all the questions.

Expect "traps"! Look for "trick" answers; answers that seem logical at first glance, but cause you to doubt; trust your instincts, again.

Revise answers; change your mind! Don't be afraid to edit your initial thinking with information gained in taking the test itself.

Figure 4.6

Unpack the Language of Directions

Identify the key words; recognize, label; highlight action words, verbs; words that tell you what to do.

Compare using synonyms; find likenesses to simple synonyms; find other words that are more concrete.

Analyze each step; take the directions apart; set a step-by-step approach; evaluate the details; note the exact instructions.

Name the skill; decide what higher order thinking you need to do; is it creative, generative thinking, or is it critical, analytical thinking?

Defend; justify; present an opinion and support it; give sensible rationale; give ample supporting documentation.

Offer a proof; show the analysis; give supporting evidence.

Trace; delineate; follow the sequence; develop a logical, simple response; show the path of your thinking.

Help define; differentiate; point out the exact nature of the word and what it calls for you to do; give critical attributes.

Illustrate; draw; show, sketch; give a telling example; use metaphors and nalogies; show through graphic representations.

Summarize; give the main idea or a synopsis; tell and retell; give a summary statement

Figure 4.7

As does any team working with a process, Data! Dialogue! Decisions! teams do, from time to time, encounter a few glitches. In this chapter, a number of frequently encountered problems are identified, and a few suggestions on how to overcome them are presented. In brief, the best advice is to use common sense, play fair, and keep truckin'!

Data! Issues

Problem.   We have too much data. How do we get started?

Solutions.   Choose the data that is going to have the largest impact on student achievement and that accurately reflects student performance. Rank the data, then choose the highest priority data.

Problem.   We don't have enough data. How do we use what we have?

Solutions.   The smallest amount of data can provide enough information to get started using the process. List additional needed information in the Dialogue! Section, What Else? Don't let this worry stop the process!

■ □ ■ □ ■

Chapter 5
Troubleshooting

Problem.   We don't have any data. What do we do?

Solutions.   No excuses! If you don't have data then make it up. Brainstorm about where the concerns are already in the district or school. Refer to the list of different data types in chapter 2. Find different sources.

Problem.   The data seems old, not reliable, or not relevant. How do we use this data?

Solutions.   Mike Schmoker says that if we wait for perfect data we will never get going. Engage in the process with the data available and take its age, reliability, or relevance into consideration the next time you discuss the results. Maybe the data will turn out to be more beneficial that you first suspected.

Dialogue! Issues

Problem.   There seems to be more finger-pointing than work. How do we move on?

Solutions.   Set the ground rules. This not the time to be pointing fingers. The purpose of this is to find a solutions and develop an action plan. Be positive! The team can make a difference!

Problem.   The team is taking too long to get started, and the conversation seems to be going nowhere. How do we get going?

■ □ ■ □ ■

Solutions.   Name a timekeeper for the group. Use
                signals to announce approaching deadlines
                to help group members stay on task. Monitor
                the amount of time each person talks.
                Structure the group dynamics for success.
                Keep it simple. If the data seem
                overwhelming, then focus on one part of one
                page. Narrow the amount of possible choices
                so that the process can begin.

Problem.   Teachers and staff form SMART goals, but the
                success of the goals is not considered in the
                next meeting. How do we move forward?

Solutions.   When we say results, we mean results.
                Results are the number one priority of any
                data dialogue. Return to the agreed on goals
                and determine how well your team did and
                how you might do differently in the future.
                Looking at data, changing instruction, and
                setting goals but then not paying attention to
                the results is like planting a garden without
                tasting the vegetables.

Problem.   There are too many unknown factors. What
                do we do?

Solutions.   Again, don't let the unknown play the most
                important role in the process. List the
                unknown to acknowledge that there was
                missing information, but press on. You can
                only change what you can control, so, if it is
                unknown, its probably out of your control.
                Remember! When all the information is not

■ □ ■ □ ■

available, make a checklist of what information is needed for the next Data! Dialogue! and Decisions! experience.

Decisions! Issues

Problem. Goals are unclear. How do we refocus?

Solutions. Stick to the SMART goal framework. It includes all the critical components needed for an effective goal. Review chapter 4 on creating SMART goals.

General Issues

Problem. There isn't enough time. How do we stretch our time?

Solutions. Use cooperative group models (see chapter 3) and ask someone to be the timer. Don't get hung up on one section of the process. Keep the process moving.

Problem. It seems to be a long time between meetings. How do we keep on course?

Solutions. Make a commitment to have meetings regularly. Schedule the times, set the time aside, and be sure to attend meetings with relevant information.

Professional Development Issues

Problem.   We already have long-term professional
                development plans. How can the decisions
                we make tie into our existing plans?

Solutions.   Evaluate and reevaluate the decisions to be
                sure the goals of the long-term professional
                development plans will increase student
                achievement. Based on the data from the
                decisions, long-term professional development
                plans will either be confirmed or will need to
                be changed.

Problem.   This is so new. How can we dovetail the
                Data! Dialogue! and Decisions! process into
                our current initiative in professional
                development?

Solutions.   Make the current initiatives available to the
                participants in the Data! Dialogue! and
                Decisions! process. Make data available that
                aligns with current initiatives.

■□■□■

Appendix A:
Data! Dialogue! Decisions! General Format

The Data

Existing Data	Observe	Analyze
Select priority data. Target data that address concerns.	Write 2–3 statements of fact about the data you have.	Analyze the data; compare, sort, notice patterns.

The Dialogue

Relevant Data	Describe	Infer
What did you find? Let the data tell the story.	**What else** do you know? Identify additional information about the situation in order to describe and analyze the data. **What else** do you *need* to know? Look for missing information about the situation to fully describe and analyze the data.	**So, what** does it mean? Discuss collaboratively. Use large charts for viewing data. Foster meaningful teamwork. Infer what the data implies.

The Decision

Relevant Data	Instructional Options	Professional Development
What did you find? Make use of the data. Do something with the information. Let the data inform classroom practice and professional development decisions.	Now, what do you need to do? What is implied or indicated by the data? How might you use it to increase student achievement? Brainstorm possible interventions based on the experts of the teacher team.	Now, what do you need to do? What is implied or indicated by the data? How might you use it to increase student achievement? Generate ideas about professional development that supports the instruction.

The Action Plan

Goal	Action	Responsibility
Now, what is the SMART goal? How might you use the data to increase student achievement? **S**pecific **M**easurable (evidence) **A**ttainable **R**esults-Oriented **T**arget Date	**Now, who** will do what? What do you need to do?	**Now, who** will do what, when? Who has responsibility for the various action steps needed?

■ □ ■ □ ■

Appendix B:
State Standards in Reading Example

	What Data... do we have?	
Data	Elementary 1-8 building ...	
	Only 22% Grade 3-6 meet or exceed national reading norms on State Standards in Reading.	
	What Else ... do we know?	**What Else** ... do we need to know?
Dialogue	-63% State Standards in Reading questions are inference questions -80% of teacher/ textbook questions are factual	Does the curriculum emphasize inference? What synonyms can be used to search for inference skills?
	So, What ... does an analysis reveal?	**So, What** ... can we infer?
	Inference word search within curriculum yields little support	Need to focus on higher order thinking (HOT) skills-inferring, drawing conclusions, hypothesizing, predicting
	Now, What ... instruction will work?	**Now, What** ... Does Professional Development (PD) supports this instruction?
Decisions	Unpack language for kids: infer-guess, draw conclusions, suggest, hint, a hunch, educated guess, beyond the given, $2 + 2 = 4$	Integrated Curriculum-how to thread the skill of inference across content

■ □ ■ □ ■

	Teach across all subjects	Brainstorm examples across content:
		Science: infer in lab work
		Social Studies: historical inferences
		Mathematics: statistical inference
		Language Arts: Read between lines ... setting characters, mood, tone
		Physical Education/Health: facial expression, body language
		Fine Arts: Infer life and times of artist
Action Plan	***What*** ... is the target goal?	***Who*** ... will do what?
	Inference skill taught in all classes; 25% increase in comprehension for Grades 3-8 on next local assessments	Grade 3-8 Staff Principal to arrange PD
	Higher Order Thinking PD	

Appendix C:
A Tale of Two City Schools

A Tale of Two City Schools:
Making the Difference With Data

R. Fogarty, D. Kinney, B. Pete, and C. Duncan

"It was the best of times, it was the worst of times," and so begins the saga of days gone by in a historical revolution in Europe, in a Dickens' classic, *A Tale of Two Cities*. And so begins the saga of days gone by in an educational revolution in America, in a data classic, *A Tale of Two City Schools*, where data, dialogue, and decisions are making the critical difference.

It is the best of times in education with standards of learning and data management technology in place. Yet, for some inner city schools, it is the worst of times in terms of the low achievement patterns that persist. The journey toward high achievement for all students is often a long and arduous one that demands the focused attention and repertoire of skills of the entire staff.

Two vignettes, DuBois Elementary School and Talcott Elementary School, both low-performing Chicago public schools, chronicle how they are moving from schools of frustration and failure to schools of slowly, steadily increasing student successes. Threaded through the tales of two city schools is a simple process that taps into Schmoker's (1996) widely accepted tenets of data-driven decision making: meaningful teamwork, managed data, and measurable goals. As you read the tales of the two

■ □ ■ □ ■

schools, notice how these fundamental principles are at work. Their stories of hard-won successes follow a simple design flow through the data phase, the dialogue phase, the decision phase that helps bring the data alive.

DuBois Elementary School Vignette

Vignette: DuBois Elementary School

DuBois Elementary School is on the southeast side of Chicago. In fact, it is about as far south and east as you can go and still be in the city. The K-8, one story building, with 485 students and 30 teachers is in the heart of the Old Riverdale neighborhood. The student population is comprised of 95.4% Black and 4.6% Hispanic students, with a 97.8% low socioeconomic demographic. Under the leadership of Principal Andrea Phifer and Assistant

DuBois Elementary School

At/Above National Norms	Reading	Growth	Math	Growth
2002	36.6	+8.4	47.6	+15.9
2001	28.2	-.6	31.7	-1.2
2000	28.8	NA	32.9	NA

Principal Vanessa Johnson, the following outlines the gains in achievement in reading and math during the past three years.

Gains in reading include a 5% increase in the top quartile, and a 10% decrease in the lowest quartile, over the past three years. In addition, an almost 50% increase in the top quartile, with a 50% decrease in lowest quartile in math, is another data-telling statement.

The Data Phase

As the principal explains, "We wanted to make growth on the Iowa Test of Basic Skills (ITBS) so we implemented a plan of quarterly local assessments to track student progress. We used the STEP Assessments provided and scored by an external partner, Kinney and Associates. But, even with the data, our scores did not improve the first year."

The assistant principal continues, "We kept the local assessments, but, we decided to wrap a professional development piece around the data management to learn more about how to use the data to inform our teaching. The statement, by Mike Schmoker, 'Even imperfect tests, and all assessments are imperfect, can promote life-changing improvements', hit home with the staff."

The Dialogue Phase

In the past, the teachers analyzed their data independently. When we moved to grade-level teams discussing the results of the local assessments and designing purposeful instruction, we started to see improvements. Mr. Wilson even took the dialogue phase to the students. He had them analyze why they had answered certain questions incorrectly. They asked, 'Was it the vocabulary? Was the wording confusing? Was it a multiple step problem?' Students began to focus on their learning and to feel like they had some control over it."

The Decision Phase

The principal adds, "After each quarterly assessment, we review the data and develop an action plan for instruction which includes specific, measurable goals and strategies the teachers will implement to improve achievement." Initially, the teachers perceived local assessments as just one more thing they to do. Now the teachers use the data as their primary manual."

The principal concludes, "Our teachers are encouraged and excited. We're not where we want to be, not by a long shot, but we can see the steady climb in the test scores and we feel like we are making headway. We're talking and we're thinking about how to make a difference. This process drives our instruction and our professional development. We know the areas we need to target for the kids and for the teachers."

Talcott Elementary School Vignette

Talcott is a huge three story building located, in Chicago's Bucktown area. While it is 80% Hispanic, it is also a melting pot with a number of other nationalities and languages all under one roof. It has 95% poverty level. The Talcott staff has been working with data from local assessments for six years. Their early results were sporadic at best, but they stuck with it and they are getting better with the process. They are approaching 50% at or above national norms in both reading and math.

■□■□■

Talcott Elementary School

At/Above National Norms	Reading	Growth	Math	Growth
2002	46.6	+9.9	47.4	+3.1
2001	36.7	4.5	44.3	-4.3
2000	41.2	+6.7	48.6	-.2
1999	34.5	+10.0	48.8	+8.0
1998	24.5	-.2	40.8	-2.0
1997	24.7	NA	42.8	NA

The Data Phase

Based on the achievement data available, the staff began to talk about instructional alignment. The data indicated unacceptable levels of achievement school-wide that persisted more two years. Only 25% of students were at or above the national norms in reading and a little more than 40% were at the same levels in mathematics.

The Dialogue Phase

Using the data, Assistant Principal Stella Vernard offered analytical prompts to begin the dialogues:

1. "What do we see indicated in the data? Are there gaps that exist between what is taught and what is prescribed by the local framework curriculum objectives."

2. "What else do we know or need to know? Are we
   testing what we are teaching? Are we teaching what
   we are testing?"

3. "So, what does it mean? Should our first step to
   increase student achievement be curriculum alignment?"

4. "Now, what do we need to do to look for alignment?
   How will we accomplish the task?"

The Decision Phase

The discussion led to the decision to use a data
management program for curriculum alignment. As part of
the process, each teacher received an "academic
roadmap" correlating teaching resources with the annual
standardized assessments. Assistant Principal Vernard
comments, "For the first time our teachers clearly saw how
the district's testing program and their classroom
instruction connected."

Continued round table dialogues brought the staff to
the next logical questions, " Have the students learned
what has been taught? How do we know what they
know? Are we getting the results we want?"

These questions led them to conclude that they
needed regular, periodic feedback on student
achievement, as opposed to waiting until the end of the
year for the results on high-stakes tests. Thus, they began
implementing quarterly local assessments in reading and
math for every student.

Talcott's teaching staff adopted a philosophy of
sharing knowledge, experiences and instructional success.
Assistant Principal Vernard reports, "While threatened at

first with a quarterly snapshot of their classes academic progress, they quickly became teaching teams using data to plan instruction. They meet quarterly to analyze the data. With the combination of teacher judgment and the quarterly assessment results, the data have allowed us to make more reliable decisions regarding instruction and individual student needs. This process ensures that no child is left behind."

The Data Phase

Data are available through demographic information that comes from the district and at the individual building level, where test scores, attendance, honors students, and cumulative folders are preserved. At the classroom level, still other information is available including teacher observations, checklists, grade books, and anecdotal reports.

With the No Child Left Behind Act of 2001, districts are required to manage data and report the data by a number of indicators: poverty, race, ethnicity, disability and limited English proficiency. In order to address these guidelines, some districts have installed sophisticated data management software systems. Both DuBois and Talcott, used components of the TIEnet Data Management System to support data disaggregation. Data available on line, any time, anywhere (with security options in place, of course) provide a viable and valuable tool that can make the difference in student achievement. Feedback is the key. Just as a heart monitor provides continuing feedback to a runner so that she may adjust her speed, exertion, and endurance levels, so does easily available student data provide ongoing feedback so that the teacher may monitor progress, adjust instruction, and reinforce gains in student achievement.

In this first phase, the educational team must delineate not only what they are looking at, but also, what they are looking for. The DuBois Elementary School faculty decided to look at their reading and math scores from the Iowa Test of Basic Skills. They were looking for patterns of strengths and weaknesses in achievement for 3rd to 8th grade.

The Dialogue Phase

It is during the dialogue phase that meaningful teams make sense of the data they have collected. As they preview, view, and review the data, experts recommend (Wellman & Lipton, 2000; Schmoker, 1996 ; Joyce & Showers, 1995) a collaborative approach to the dialogue by displaying the data on large charts to facilitate robust discussions. This keeps the focus on problem solving for school improvement and increasing student achievement, rather than on evaluative judgments about staff.

Four fundamental questions promote rich dialogues: What? What else? So, What? and Now, what?

What? What does the team see? What data are striking? What patterns emerge? What data support issues and/or concern areas? What data are surprising? Confusing? At this point the team tries to describe the data as thoroughly and accurately as possible using charts, maps, and notes to draw the emerging the picture. DuBois looked at percentages of students that met, exceeded or did not meet the national norms in reading and math during a three-year period, while Talcott analyzed gaps in their curriculum.

What else? What else do the teachers know that informs the data they see? What other data impact on the patterns revealed in the new data? Do new data support the findings or invalidate what the team sees? What else does the team need to know that is missing from the available data? What collateral information is needed to confirm or disavow the patterns that seem to be revealed in the targeted data? As "people closest to the problem", (Deming,1986), these teams are the ones most aware and most informed of related aspects. Their observations, their knowledge, their insights create a richer story of what the data tell. The DuBois staff decision about tapping into teacher expertise led to great increases in their math test scores.

So, What? So, what does it mean? What is implied? What can be inferred from the complete picture of the available data? What conclusions can be drawn that are logical and supported by the evidence? The team tries to make sense of the patterns that emerge. This phase is not about "jumping to conclusions," rather it is about drawing conclusions in logical, reasonable, commonsense ways; understanding what the data suggest; validating what is revealed through the data. It is here that the team considers instructional strategies (Marzano et al., 2001) and professional development (Joyce and Showers, 1995) options. The DuBois staff determined that just having the data available had not been enough to produce significant change in student achievement. They decided they needed professional development on data-driven decision making to understand what to do with the data. This turned out to be a key insight culled from their dialogues.

Now, what? Now, what decisions can be made? Now, what plans can be outlined? Now, what action(s) can be taken? What interventions can be initiated? What kinds of support might teachers need? As they try to make sense of what they see, what they know, and what they suspect, the questions propel the team toward mindful decisions. The Talcott staff inferred from their static test data that they needed to know how well their curriculum was aligned with the assessments.

In this dialogue, each question deepens and/or broadens the search for relevant, meaningful clues to increased student achievement.

The Decision Phase

The overriding goal of this entire process is to inform instructional practice with data- driven decisions. This third phase of decision-making leads the teams into brainstorm mode, as they tap into their pool of instructional. It is during this phase that the team sets specific, measurable goals. These goals are designed to yield relevant, real, and rapid results that indicate that progress is being made; that positive changes are occurring and that the team is getting the results envisioned. Talcott focused on curriculum alignment and periodic local assessments to help monitor the emerging picture and guide the adjustments needed in the curriculum.

The final phase of the data-driven decision-making is at the heart of the process. During the decision phase, teams must ask themselves the central question, "Are we getting the results we want?" If the answer is, "Yes," then they must keep on doing what they're doing...whatever it is that is working and then, they must with continue the data, dialogue, and decision cycle with the next relevant focus.

But, if the answer is "No," if they are not getting the results they envisioned and if they are not meeting their goals, then adjustments must be made and new plans laid.

The Difference: Data! Dialogue! Decisions!

The Data Phase
Select priority data. Target data that address concerns.

Observe
Observe the available data picture. Preview, view, and review the data that target the priority concerns and concerns that are on the agenda.

Determine what you are looking at and what you are looking for?

Connect to new data to past/current concerns.

Decide what data are needed and what you plan to do with the data; manage the data you have (Schmoker,1996) as skillfully as possible.

Analyze
Analyze by looking for strengths and weaknesses. What jumps out? What data are missing?

Scan for patterns in the data. Create general categories. Create more specific labels.

Compare and contrast with previous data for gains or slips.

Start to chart the information. Use a graphic to represent the data the team sees. Look for trend lines. Record findings from the round table dialogues.

The Dialogue Phase
Let the data tell the story of the school, the class or the student.

Describe
Ask four questions:
What did you find?
Describe the existing data in some detail. Connect to previous data. Look for growth patterns.

What else do you know or need to know? Look for additional information about the situation in order to describe and analyze the data.

Infer
Begin with data statements that are quantifiable. Use the data judiciously. Find the glaring concerns that are fully supported by the data.

Try to complete the data picture with missing information and/or complementary data.

So, what does it mean? Discuss collaboratively. Use large charts for viewing data. Foster meaningful teamwork (Schmoker, 1996)

Then, go beyond the given data and infer some things. Draw some conclusions. Create hypotheses. Make some best guesses. Honor intuitive hunches.

Now, what do you need to do? What is implied indicated by the data? How might you use it to increase student achievement?

Keep trying to make sense of the data picture. Use the experience and expertise and the common sense of the team.

The Decision Phase

Make use of the data. Do something with the information. Let the data inform classroom practice and professional development decisions.

Instructional Decisions

As a teaching team, tap into the talents and resources of a caring staff.

Prioritize all possible strategies that might impact on the target concern that emerged from the data. Use the data picture to problem solve and to select the interventions to be used.

Set a measurable goal with a schedule for monitoring and set a reasonable deadline to check progress and to evaluate results.

Implement the target ideas. Monitor progress. Adjust as needed. Look for "rapid results" (Schmoker, 1996).

Professional Development Decisions

Determine what kind of professional development support is needed to implement the intervention(s).

Decide what the teachers might need to know and be able to do, in order to fully implement the plan.

Decide how the professional development might be delivered to relevant staff; how teachers might experience meaningful, job-embedded models that help them implement the target behaviors.

Take action with the professional development as it drives the instructional interventions.

■ ☐ ■ ☐ ■

Appendix D: People Search

People Search: Data/Technology

Find someone who:

1. Admits to having abandoned a piece of exercise equipment and will give some reasons.

2. Can share a good idea for motivating teachers about data and technology.

3. Will share an on-line search that gave them with interesting results.

4. Will compare and contrast a job done by hand and now done on-line or with the use of computer technology.

5. Counts calories (or carbohydrates or points) and will explain why.

6. Can explain and will justify how they select the "essential standards" from the "supplemental standards" at their grade level or in their discipline.

7. Complete the analogy: Technology:Data: ____:____.

8. Ranks the following the same as you do.

____Grow Network

____State Test Scores

____Local Assessments

____Standardized Test Scores

■□■□■

Bibliography

American College Test. (2003). *ACT Web Site*. Available: www.act.org

Amrein, A. L., & Berliner, D.C. (2003). The effects of high-stakes testing on student motivation and learning. *Educational Leadership, 60*(5), 32–38.

Armstrong, T. (1999). *Seven kinds of smart: Identifying and developing your multiple intelligences*. New York: Penguin Putnam.

Baldrige. (2003). *Baldrige Web Site*. Available: www.baldrige.com

Barell, J. (1998). *PBL: Problem based learning: An inquiry approach*. Thousand Oaks, CA: Corwin.

Barton, M. L., Heidema, C., & Jordan, D. (2002). Teaching reading in mathematics and science. *Educational Leadership, 60*(3), 24–28.

Bell, L. (2002). Strategies that close the gap. *Educational Leadership, 60*(4), 32–34.

Bellanca, J. (1997). *Active learning handbook for the multiple intelligences classroom*. Thousand Oaks, CA: Corwin.

Bellanca, J., & Fogarty, R. (2003). *Blueprints for achievement in the cooperative classroom* (3rd ed.). Thousand Oaks, CA: Corwin.

Berman, S. (1997). *Project learning*. Thousand Oaks, CA: Corwin.

■□■□■

Berman, S. (1999). *Service learning*. Thousand Oaks, CA: Corwin.

Bernhardt, V. L. (2000). Intersections. *Journal of Staff Development, 21*(1), 33–36.

Bernhardt, V. L. (2003). No schools left behind. *Educational Leadership, 60*(5), 26–30.

Bradley, A. (1999). Zeroing in on teachers. *Education Week, 18*(17), 46–52.

Brady, M. (2000). The standards juggernaut. *Phi Delta Kappan, 81*(9), 649–651.

Bonstingl, J. J. (1992). The total quality classroom. *Educational Leadership, 49*(6), 66–70.

Bonstingl, J. J. (1993). The quality movement: What's it really about? *Educational Leadership, 51*(1), 66.

Burke, K. (1999). *How to assess authentic learning*. Thousand Oaks, CA: Corwin.

Burke, K., Fogarty, R., & Belgrade, S. (1994). *The portfolio connection*. Thousand Oaks, CA: Corwin.

Caine, R. N., & Caine, G. (1991). *Making connections: Teaching and the human brain*. Menlo Park, CA: Addison-Wesley.

Carnavale, A. (2003, April 23). Poor and minority highschoolers find rigorous courses to be exclusive. *Education Week*, pp. 1, 14–16.

Cawelti, G. (2003). Lessons from research that changed education. *Educational Leadership, 60*(5), 18–21.

■□■□■

Conzemius, A. (2000). Framework. *Journal of Staff Development, 21*(1), 38–41.

Costa, A. (1991). *School as a home for the mind.* Thousand Oaks, CA: Corwin.

Csikszentmihalyi, M. (1990). *Flow: The psychology of optimal experience.* New York: Harper and Row.

Deming, W. E. (1986). *Out of the crisis.* Cambridge, MA: MIT Press.

Dewey, J. (1938). *Experience and education.* New York: Collier.

Dickens, C. (1859). *A tale of two cities.* New York: Vintage Classics.

Eisner, E. W. (1979). *Educational imagination: On the design and evaluation of school programs.* New York: Macmillan.

Feurstein, R. (1979). *Instrumental enrichment.* Baltimore: University Park Press.

Fogarty, R. (1990). *Designs for cooperative interactions.* Thousand Oaks, CA: Corwin.

Fogarty, R. (1997). *Problem based learning and other curriculum models for the multiple intelligences classroom.* Thousand Oaks, CA: Corwin.

Fogarty, R. (1998). *Balanced assessments.* Thousand Oaks, CA: Corwin.

Fogarty, R. (2001a). *Finding the time and the money for professional development.* Chicago: Fogarty & Associates.

Fogarty, R. (2001b). *Literacy matters.* Arlington Heights, IL: Skylight Professional Development.

Fogarty, R. (2001c). *Making sense of the research on the brain and learning.* Chicago: Fogarty & Associates.

Fogarty, R. (2001d). *A model for mentoring our teachers: Centers of pedagogy.* Chicago: Fogarty & Associates.

Fogarty, R. (2001e). *Student learning standards: A blessing in disguise.* Chicago: Fogarty & Associates.

Fogarty, R. (2001f). *Teachers make a the difference.* Chicago: Fogarty & Associates.

Fogarty, R. (2001g). *Ten things new teachers need to succeed.* Thousand Oaks, CA: Corwin.

Fogarty, R. (2002a). *Brain compatible classroom* (2nd ed.). Thousand Oaks, CA: Corwin.

Fogarty , R. (2002b). *How to integrate the curricula* (2nd ed.). Thousand Oaks, CA: Corwin.

Fogarty, R. J., & Pete, B. M. (2003). *Nine best practices that make the difference.* Thousand Oaks, CA: Corwin.

Fogarty, R., & Stoehr, J. (1995). *Integrating the curricula with multiple intelligences.* Thousand Oaks, CA: Corwin.

Fullan, M., & Stiegelbauer, S. (1999). *The new meaning of educational change.* New York: Teachers College Press.

Gardner, H. (1983). *Frames of mind: The theory of multiple intelligences.* New York: Basic Books.

Gardner, H. (1999). *Intelligence reframed: Multiple intelligences for the 21st century.* New York: Basic Books.

Gehring, J. (2002, June 12). Ohio faces up to new achievement gap data. *Education Week,* pp. 1–3. Retrieved 21 November 2002 from www.edweek.org

Gratz, D. B. (2000). High standards for whom? *Phi Delta Kappan, 81*(9), 681–687.

■ □ ■ □ ■

Guskey, T. R. (2003). How classroom assessments improve learning. *Educational Leadership, 60*(5), 6–11.

Hart, B., & Risley, T. (2003, Spring). The early catastrophe: The 30 million word gap by age 3. *The American Educator,* pp. 1–8. Retrieved 23 April 2003 from www.aft.org/americaneducator/spring2003/catastrophe.html

Haycock, K. (1999, March). *Good teaching matters ... a lot.* NSDC Results, 45–46.

Haycock, K. (2001). Closing the achievement gap. *Educational Leadership, 58*(6), 6–11.

Hunter, M. (1970). *Transfer.* El Segundo, CA: TIP.

Johnson, D., Johnson, R., & Holubec, E. (1986). *Circles of learning: Cooperation in the classroom.* Alexandria, VA: Association for Supervision and Curriculum Development.

Joyce, B. (1999). The great literacy problem and success for all. *Phi Delta Kappan, 81*(2), 129–131.

Joyce, B., & Showers, B. (1995) *Student achievement through staff development: Fundamentals of school renewal.* White Plaines, NY: Longman.

Kagan, S. (1990). *Cooperative learning resources for teachers.* San Juan Capistrano, CA: Resources for Teachers.

Kohn, A. (1999, May). The dark side of standards. *Education Update,* p. 7.

Kohn, A. (1999, December 9). Tests that cheat students. *New York Times,* OP-ED, p. A31.

Lazear, D. (1999). *Eight ways of knowing* (3rd ed.). Thousand Oaks, CA: Corwin.

■ □ ■ □ ■

Lyman, F., & McTighe, J. (1998). Cueing thinking in the classroom: The promise of theory-embedded tools. *Educational Leadership, 45*(7), 18–24.

Marzano, R. (2003). Using data: Two wrongs and a right. *Educational Leadership, 60*(5), 56–60.

Marzano, R., Pickering, D., & McTighe, J. (1997). *Assessing student outcomes.* Alexandria, VA: Association for Supervision and Curriculum Development.

Marzano, R., Pickering, D. & Pollock, J. (2001). *Classroom instruction that works.* Alexandria, VA: Association for Supervision and Curriculum Development.

Menéndez, R. (Writer/Director), & Musca, T. (Writer). (1988). *Stand and deliver* [Motion picture]. United States: Warner Home Video.

No Child Left Behind Act of 2001. (2001). Washington, DC: U.S. Department of Education. Available from http://www.ed.gov/nclb/

Parsons, B. (2003). A tale of two schools' data. *Educational Leadership, 60*(5), 66–68.

Reeves, D. (2003). 101 questions and answers about standards. Retrieved 12 December 2003 from http://www.makingstandardswork.com

Rose, L., & Gallup, A. M. (1999). The 31st annual Phi Delta Kappa/Gallup Poll of the public's attitudes toward the public schools [Insert]. *Phi Delta Kappan, 81*(1), 41–56.

Schmoker, M. (1996). *Results: The key to continuous school improvement.* Alexandria, VA: Association for Supervision and Curriculum Development.

■ □ ■ □ ■

Schmoker, M. (1999a). *Results: The key to continuous school improvement* (2nd ed.). Alexandria, VA: Association for Supervision and Curriculum Development.

Schmoker, M. (1999b, November 3). The quiet revolution in achievement. *Education Week*, pp. 1–4. Retrieved 22 February, 2002 from www.edweek.org

Schmoker, M. (2000). The results we want. *Educational Leadership, 57*(5), 62–65.

Schmoker, M. (2001). *The results field book.* Alexandria, VA: Association for Supervision and Curriculum Development.

Schmoker, M., & Marzano, R. (1999). Realizing the promise of standards-based education. *Educational Leadership, 56*(6), 17–21.

Slavin, R. E. (2003). A reader's guide to scientifically-based research. *Educational Leadership, 60*(5), 12–16.

Sparks, D. 2000. Results are the reason: Interview with Mike Schmoker. *Journal of Staff Development, 21*(1), 51–53.

Sylwester, R. (1998). *Student brains, school issues: A collection.* Thousand Oaks, CA: Corwin.

Taylor, B. M., Pearson, P. D., Peterson, D. S., & Rodriguez, M. C. (in press). Reading growth in high-poverty classrooms: The influence of teacher practices that encourage cognitive engagement in literacy learning. *The Elementary School Journal.*

Tomlinson, C. A. (1999a). *The differentiated classroom: Responding to the needs of all learners.* Alexandria, VA: Association for Supervision and Curriculum Development.

Tomlinson, C. A. (1999b). Mapping a route toward differentiated curriculum. *Educational Leadership, 57*(1), 12–16.

■ □ ■ □ ■

Tomlinson, C. A. (2000). *Reconcilable differences? Standards-based teaching and differentiation*. Alexandria, VA: Association for Supervision and Curriculum Development.

U.S. Department of Education. (1993). *Adult literacy in America*. Retrieved 24 April, 2003 from http://www.firstbook.org/about/factsonilliteracy.shtml

U.S. Department of Education. (2003). *Overview*. Retrieved 12 December, 2003 from http://www.ed.gov/nclb/overview/intro/index.html

Vacca , R. T. (2002).From efficient decoders to strategic readers. *Educational Leadership, 60*(3), 6–11.

Viadero, D. (2000, March 22). Lags in minority achievement defy traditional explanations. *Education Week*, pp. 1–8.

Wellman, B., & Lipman, L. (2000). Navigation: Creating a path through a sea of information. *Journal of Staff Development, 21*(1), 47–50.

Wiggins, G., & McTighe, J. (1998). *Understanding by design*. Alexandria, VA: Association for Supervision and Curriculum Development.

Zemelman, S., Daniels, H., & Hyde, A. (1998). *Best practice: New standards for teaching and learning in American schools*. Portsmouth, NH: Heinemann.

Teachers Make a the Difference

The good teacher *instructs,*
　　the excellent teacher *invites,*
　　　　the superior teacher *involves,*
　　　　　　the great teacher *inspires.*

Robin Fogarty—Chicago, 1999

The Corwin logo—a raven striding across an open book—represents the union of courage and learning. Corwin is committed to improving education for all learners by publishing books and other professional development resources for those serving the field of PreK–12 education. By providing practical, hands-on materials, Corwin continues to carry out the promise of its motto: **"Helping Educators Do Their Work Better."**